# Paris in 3 Days

## The Definitive Tourist Guide Book That Helps You Travel Smart and Save Time

There are many types of tourists guides and some of them focus on Paris, but this book will prove incredibly helpful thanks to its high practical value. It is a guide that was primarily designed for people who have to stay in Paris for a few days only. It is for them that it comes hardest to organize their visit in the city, because they basically have to make many choices and 'condense' the beauty of Paris in a short time frame. However, naturally this book is also useful for people whose stay in the capital is longer, but who don't know very well what is worth seeing most of all, what they should do in Paris to get around easily, and how they could save time and maybe also money.

Here is a preview of what you will learn in this guide:

- what makes Paris so attractive for tourists and what is particular about it

- key information about Paris

- how to get there

- tips on means of transport in the city

- advice on accommodation

- highly recommended touristic attractions that are a must even if you stay only 3 days

- tips on what and where to eat/drink if you want to experience a typically French flavor or interesting places in the capital

- what you should see if you're interested in culture and entertainment

- recommendations for specific events that your stay can synchronize with

Why do you think Oscar Wilde said: "When good Americans die, they go to Paris?" This guide offers you information about the most important touristic highlights in Paris. Such places include historical monuments, places that have high architectural or artistic value, and social attractions. Many of these places are already landmarks, but this guide aims at helping you organize your trip by including only what is really a must-see attraction. This guide also provides many useful tips on what you shouldn't miss in Paris if you're interested in cultural life such as theater, concerts, or art galleries. Moreover, it advises you on what you should consider from a practical perspective if you want to have a smooth ride through the city and not spend the highest amount of money. This short guide is designed for people of all ages and for this reason it presents a wide array of details and information that anyone can benefit from. This book also recommends a few basic facts to consider during your trip, from tipping habits to things that you can benefit from if you purchase a Paris pass. Paris surely offers a memorable experience to anyone who knows how to travel intelligently, saving time and unwanted expenses. Enjoy it and make the best of your visit!

# Table of Contents

# 1. Introduction

Paris is a city with a multifaceted history as well as a rich artistic and cultural life. The city is definitely one of Europe's main touristic attractions that even people from various continents long to visit and come to see. However, many of those who know Paris have very surprising and interesting reactions to it. Some people immediately fall in love with Paris and its youthful and creative atmosphere. Others experience a form of disappointment when faced with a concrete Paris that may not be the same with the romanticized Paris they know from the web, from postcards, or just other people's stories.

While this guide only aims at drawing some broad lines to help you understand what's unique and appealing about Paris, it is surely interesting to take you through people's images of Paris, too. This book will provide you with the most useful information about one of Europe's most fascinating places that many writers or painters haven't left unnoticed or unmentioned. What do you need to know if you have to spend a short time in Paris? Can you cover the main attractions and landmarks in just 3 days? What shouldn't you miss? What do you need to make your trip and your stay easier? Where can you eat and drink if you want to taste some of the Parisian flavor? These are only some of the questions that you'll find answers to through this travel guide. This book is exactly what you need if you want to discover Paris in a practical and intelligent way.

Besides the most important touristic data that anyone visiting Paris needs, you will also get a feel about the French capital after reading this book. What kind of atmosphere does one find in Paris? Is there an old Paris, a city from 'once upon a time' that still maintains an air of mystery or fantasy? Many people are captivated by the French capital and consider it unique and hard to equal by another city. To help you understand how poignant the impression Paris leaves on us can be, let's just recall the words of Hemingway himself in one of his famous novels: 'If you are lucky enough to have lived in Paris as a young man, then wherever you go for the rest of your life, it stays with you, for Paris is a movable feast.' This is very close to what even people who visit Paris as tourists confess. They often talk about a memorable impression that makes them long to return into the city. In case you wonder why Paris is so striking and unforgettable, the answer comes down to a myriad of landmarks and places that charm people and can transport them back in time through their rich background. In Paris, history becomes movable and art helps you understand it directly through an immediate contact with the ages and places it evokes. There's hardly anything cold and detached in Paris. The charm of this city has a lot to do with an atmosphere that appears emotionally charged and can make people experience things subjectively. Paris is hardly a place you explore with a strictly cold mind.

To help you grasp the uniqueness of the French capital better, let's just say there is deep truth in the words of Victor Hugo who said that he who contemplates the depth of Paris is seized with vertigo. In the writer's words: "nothing is more fantastic. Nothing is more tragic. Nothing is more sublime." While you will definitely grasp this chic-tragic blend of Paris when stepping into the capital and exploring its streets, architecture, restaurants, and venues, this guide will open up a few doors for you to help you understand why Paris is so easy to love. So that you don't simply fall head over heels in love with this city, you will also find a lot of practical information in the following pages to help you make the right decisions.

# 2. Key Information about Paris

## Money Matters

It may be charming to forget about money while visiting Paris, but let's stay realistic and sort out a few things every tourist needs to know. The official currency of France is the Euro since 2002. This will make things very easy to get around in a relaxed way, especially if you're from a Western European country. Otherwise you should know you can exchange money in every bank in France in accordance with the currency and conversion rates that correspond to your country and time of visit. There are also ATMs in many public places. You can use them to withdraw money directly in euro. However keep in mind certain banks charge fairly high fees for international transactions (e.g. even around 7 eu for a reasonable sum of 100 eu). Ideally you should exchange money. Alternatively, you can also use a card such as Visa, Mastercard, or American Express. These types of card are widely accepted around Paris in malls, restaurants, travel points, or hotels, especially in very central parts of the city.

# Tipping in Paris

In Paris there is a service charge of 15% of the overall price that you will usually find included in your bill in most bars, cafes, and restaurants. However, you can always leave some extra tip if you were absolutely pleased with the service or the person you dealt with. There will be no problem if you don't: this part is up to you. You can leave a few euros (or around 5% of the sum) in restaurants and a few extra cents to round things up when you have drinks. For taxis you should tip more. The general rule is 10% of the trip's price. You should also keep in mind to leave around 1 euro for your room service or porter. In other places such as the hairstylist's, you should tip about 10 % for excellent service. The likelihood of going to a hairdresser as a tourist, however, is quite small.

## The Paris Pass

Although Paris is not the most expensive capital in Europe, there are no reasons why you shouldn't want to take advantage of the opportunity of saving a little money. The Paris pass comes in several versions and forms to suit your needs. You can purchase one for 2, 4, or 6 days, depending on how long you plan to stay. At the same time, you can get a Museum Pass, an Attraction Pass, and even a transport pass. Choose what you like most and you'll surely save money! Instead of paying about 20 euro or more for a ticket to every museum and famous place, you can purchase a pass that includes Louvre, Versailles, a cruise, one day on the hop off bus tour, and many others. You'll pay 180-220 euros for 4-6 days and you'll be able to have an inclusive and cost-effective visit in Paris.

# 3. Transport to and in Paris

There are 2 major airports in Paris: Charles de Gaulle and Orly. The biggest one is Charles de Gaulle where you can find many international and domestic flights in a very dynamic and modern atmosphere. However, the place is quite far from the city center, 23 km northeast of the city. There are several ways to get to the center without any problem, but you should consider spending a bit more time on the road. There are buses that connect the airport to the city. They run every 30 minutes and can take passengers from various terminals. Tickets will cost you about 10 euros. Alternatively, you can take the regional train and get to major points in Paris in about 30-45 minutes. Costs vary from 3-4 euros per ticket (which corresponds to specific zones) to 8 euros for the RER B and airport shuttle variant. The cheapest way is using the RER trains which will take you to an important part of the city, Gare de Nord, in about 30 minutes. You can use the metro or the tram from there to get to your destination. In case you prefer entering Paris majestically by taxi, you are welcome to spend 50-60 euros and dedicate almost an hour of your life to this adventure.

As for Orly, if you land in this airport, you'll have an easier way out and into the heart of Paris. You will only have to pay for one tram ticket and one metro ticket, which will be about 4 euros. Tramway 7 will take you to the metro line with the same number and you'll thus get to central places in Paris without spending much time or effort. The means of transport for this route run quite often and make for a very comfortable journey through Paris.

How about getting from a foreign country to one of the airports of Paris? You can benefit from the services of the largest French airline, Air France, a company that has flights in both Orly and Charles de Gaulle. However, should you want to travel low-cost for one reason or another, you can count on other European airlines that have good connections with Paris from various places (often capitals). For instance, consider German Wings, Easy Jet, and Ryanair. You will be able to enjoy both comfort and a cost-effective flight.

How does one get around the city as a tourist? Paris is quite large and it's surely worth visiting many places. Depending on the length of your stay, you can purchase a 10-ticket package, so that you can use the tram for several trips during a few days. In Paris you'll get to many areas quite easily by traveling either by tram, or by metro ...and sometimes you'll have to resort to both means of transport, especially if you stay farther from the city center. The easiest and most inexpensive way to get around, the 10-trip package, will cost around 14 euros, while 1 ticket only is almost 2 euros. For tourists who intend to stay longer in the city and move around more, a one-day ticket might be a good alternative. Choose yours depending on the city zone you have your accommodation in and what you plan to visit. You will have the option to pay for free access to either 2, or 3 zones. The price for 3 zones is almost 10 euros, while the other ticket (more tourist-friendly) is around 7 euros. There are 5 zones in Paris, but you are very unlikely to need to visit all of them. What you should keep in mind in case you don't purchase a daily ticket is the fact that one tram/bus trip should take less than 30 minutes; otherwise you'll have to pay for a second tickct, as one ticket is only valid for this limited interval.

If you are not constrained by certain factors, you can purchase the Paris International Card which will allow you free traveling around the city for 1, 2, 3, and even 5 days in any zone. How much will it cost you? For adults the price starts from around 24 euros and it reaches a rather comfortable and practical level of 50 euros for 3 days. In case you plan to stay longer, you can always buy the 5-day card which costs around 60 euros. As you can see, it doesn't have to cost a lot just because you want to explore one of Europe's most fascinating and maybe even most expensive cities in certain respects.

# 4. Accommodation

Where in Paris should you stay? How much will it be? A luxury hotel will lure you with amazing eye-watering prices. If this is absolutely fine with you, choose places such as the Mandarin Hotel or the Ritz and be ready to pay 500-1000 euros per night for 5-star "facilities". If you are only looking for a 3-star place and you would also like to enjoy a more romantic atmosphere, go for Hotel du Levant or Hotel d'Amour. A room is 100-150 euros per night. Such places can be great choices for a honeymoon or another kind of celebration, for instance. Maybe you want something near the Eiffel Tour... In this case, don't hesitate to book a room in Hotel Eiffel Saint Charles. Other great options in terms of location are Central Hotel Paris, Hotel Louvre Rivoli, Europe Hotel, or Best Western Hotel Star Champs Elysees.

What about budget accommodation? How low on your budget can you go if you want to visit Paris? The truth is Paris is a rather expensive city and even in a 2-star hotel you will have to pay over 35 euros per night. Consider Villa Fenelon, Bonsejour Montmartre, Hotel de la Place des Alpes, Hotel Bonne Nouvelle, Hotel Jarry, Hotel de l'Europe, Timhotel Montmartre etc. You may be able to get a central location for 50 euros/night. It's a bit better if you are in a couple and you need a double room, in which case you can get away with 70-80 euros even in a gorgeous place in Paris that will make traveling and visiting the city quite practical.

# 5. Sightseeing

When you have only 3 days on your hands, it's not easy to select only the "la crème de la crème" for your visit, as the French would say. So how can you avoid missing out on the essence of Paris through its attractions, architecture, and culture? This chapter will help you out and indicate top must-see places that will make your stay in the French capital totally unforgettable.

## Notre-Dame de Paris

This architectural gem is surely one of the most valuable landmarks of the city of Paris. It dates from the 12th century and it employs a superb Gothic style. Its allure is an imposing and majestic one that creates a unique atmosphere, whether you are a Catholic, or not. Its stained glass masterpieces are quite renowned all over the world and seeing them in real life is definitely an artistic treat. For a more sensational experience, you should climb the 400 steps to get to the top of the towers.

## The Eiffel Tower

Certainly *the* symbol of Paris from the most touristic viewpoint possible, this construction would probably not be as fantastic artistically speaking if it didn't offer people the possibility of a splendid panoramic view over the city. The tower is over 300 meters high and it is definitely worth paying something to take the lift to the top and reign over Paris ... at least visually. Most people who think they don't have time for such an adventure usually regret it.

## La Sainte Chapelle

This marvelous cathedral is not far from Notre Dame. It dates from the 13th century and it is built in royal Gothic style. It is part of the Capetian royal palace whose construction was ordered by French royalties. It is located in the heart of Paris, namely on the Ile de la Cite. You cannot miss the gorgeous stained glass that makes it extremely valuable artistically speaking – one of France's most precious treasures. It is one of the most remarkable stained glass collections in the world.

# The Arc De Triomphe

The most imposing and interesting arch in the world, this construction was meant to mark the memory of people who fought in the Napoleonic wars. The arch was built in the 19th century and it is an authentic historical monument. Although as a tourist you are likely to be interested in its image and remarkable position on the streets of France rather than in raw historical data, it is actually worth noticing all the names that are engraved on the arch. They designate many names of generals as well as the wars they fought in. The majestic arch is located in the famous Place Charles de Gaulle, towards the Western end of Champs-Elysees. A patient walk along the famous "fancy" boulevard can certainly be topped with the sight of this historical place.

## Champs-Elysees

This avenue is not only beautiful as a site of major social activity, but also totally recommendable if you are interested in classy shopping and modern high quality stores and brands. Along this street you can also find cafes, cinemas, and bars that will certainly make your stay in Paris more chic and pleasant. Watch out for prices though: this area is one of the most expensive in Paris and probably in the whole world (both in terms of services and goods and when it comes to real estate matters).

## Sacre-Coeur

This white and delicate-looking church crowns the Montmartre area that no tourist can miss. It is built in Roman-Catholic style and it dates from the 19th century. It is doubtlessly worth seeing after you visit the famous French district and climb the many stairs that lead you to the top of Montmartre. This is one of the most active and "alive" places in Paris and it's always likely to find yourself in a sea of tourists "swarming" towards the sacred heart of the French capital. The sight of this church is interesting even before you get to it. Moreover, if you climb to the top of the dome, you can enjoy a marvelous panoramic view of Paris from one of its highest places (the second after the Eiffel Tower). The inner part of the church may not be as spectacular as Notre Dame, but the rest of the setting and the architectural value are fantastic.

## Place Vêndome

This is one of the most famous and beautiful squares in Europe. It dates from the 18th century, but many changes have been made throughout the years in this place. What you can see now is the impressive Vêndome Column which commemorates Napoleon's victory in the battle of Austerlitz. This square cannot be missed, especially since it's located near the Tuileries Gardens and it's well-known for its luxury hotels such as the Ritz or Hotel de Boulogne.

## Montmartre

This renowned district with a long history of its own is one of the most fabulous and dynamic places in the French capital. It has traditionally been a "hub" for high art and famous artists, although nowadays you can also find less elitist kind of works (for more commercial reasons that are not hard to understand). Important personalities such as Dali, Picasso, Mondrian, and Van Gogh have lived and worked in Montmartrc. Apart from being a historic space one cannot miss when visiting Paris, this district can also offer you the opportunity to dine in fine restaurants right in the heart of the capital and its fervent artistic life. If you don't want to miss such experiences and memories, you might want to add a few euros to what you planned to spend for lunch or dinner and enjoy a meal in Montmartre.

## The Latin Quarter

Although this might be an attraction that draws younger people who want to immerse in a similarly youthful and vivacious atmosphere, you are welcome to visit this part of Paris where the famous Sorbonne University is located. This district won't offer you many architectural landmarks apart from that, but it will certainly win you over with its student life and myriad of pubs and bistros. Besides, you can also check out some other educational institutions in the area such as the Schola Cantorum or the Pantheon-Assas University.

## The Tuileries Gardens

These beautiful gardens were designed in the 17th century by the landscape artist André le Nôtre who also created the plan for the Versailles gardens. There are many statues in these gardens that you will surely enjoy seeing as you walk through the marvelous and elegantly shaped surroundings. Some of these statues were damaged in the 2nd World War and subsequently restored. Among the famous and extremely valuable statues in Tuileries you will have the chance to see Rodin's The Kiss and Eve. In this place you can resort to more "mundane" relaxation and entertainment methods, too: you can lounge in the sun in a metal chair next to the large fountain in the gardens or you can rent a toy sailboat.

## Bois de Boulogne

Another important park in Paris and one of the most interesting in Europe, Bois de Boulogne is great to visit especially after you've filled your day(s) with more cultural places and events. You will have the opportunity to ride in a horse-driven carriage that will remind you of times long gone or you can just dine in one of the luxurious (and expensive) restaurants in this park. In case you're visiting Paris during the summer and you are in the mood for a picnic, this is the place to be! A zoo and an amusement park are also available as a part of the larger Bois de Boulogne, which you will find worthwhile, especially if you have kids.

## The Pantheon

This mausoleum is one of the most visible landmarks in the French capital. It was initially a church, but it was later turned into a national mausoleum. This is the place where you can find tombs of famous French personalities such as

Hugo, Zola, or Voltaire. This place is interesting to visit and watch from the outside, given its high architectural value. However, if you are curious and you enjoy a darker and emptier place, you are free to go inside, too. You will also have the chance to see many large paintings representing important moments in the history of France.

## Palais Royale

You can visit this place with great historical value and enchanting gardens if you are near the Louvre museum. It was built during the time of Cardinal Richelieu in the 18th century. Inside you can find many rooms that evoke French history as well as various shops in the arcades. The sight might be better to watch though – these shops are quite expensive and not overly practical. But if you are a fan of antique toys and stamps, it will be a pleasure to check out the stores. Otherwise you can dine in the luxury restaurants in the Palais Royal or just visit the installation in the cour d'honeur (on the south end) whose columns with black and white strips have become an important sight in Paris. This installation was designed by Daniel Buren and they add an element of minimalism and modernity in an otherwise historic and luxurious place.

# 6. Eat&Drink

If you want to explore French cuisine and don't care about prices too much, you sure have many options in Paris. But let's stop at a few places that are quite appreciated by a wide variety of people from many countries, of many ages, and belonging to various walks of life. At least once anyone can afford fine dining in the French capital, can't they?

L'Auberge du 15 is a quite place that's not located right in the most hectic area of Paris. It's not very large and it evokes a farmhouse atmosphere. You can eat a meal for 50 euros or more, but there's also a fixed menu for lunch that lets you get away with about 30 per person. Here you can enjoy various chestnut dishes, lamb, foie gras in cabbage leaves, or a more classic veal served with vegetables. In any case, it's a great place for French cuisine at its best and most genuine.

Le Train Bleu is a luxury restaurant whose atmosphere and food can make you feel like a bona fide aristocrat. Vintage frescos and fine traditional French cuisine go very well served with quality wine. Expect to leave after paying minimum 50-60 euros for a full meal in this place. When only a bottle of wine costs 25-30 euros, does that sound too much? It's worth the whole effort though, if you want to taste lobster served on salad and dressed in walnut oil or the typically French veal topped with delicious fine cheese.

A more fancy option, albeit a more expensive one is Le Joules Verne, a restaurant located about 120 meters up the Eiffel Tour. A splendid view, exquisite food, and a romantic atmosphere are only a few of the benefits of dining in this place. Keep in mind that the place is quite high-style, which means you have to go there dressed elegantly and prepared to pay a lot for a meal. How much? A lunch menu is 90-100 euros, but it might be totally worth the opportunity to eat out (or up) in one the top restaurants in the French capital.

Septime is a more accessible place with a modern vibe that works if you don't like heavy or pompous restaurants. This is a good alternative to pricey and very classy places where you have to go with a stuffed wallet. Here you can enjoy a more minimalistic and casual atmosphere and amazing food for a reasonable price. You can eat delicious seafood, for instance, while you pay only about 30 euros for lunch. How does that sound?

Last, but not least, people who travel on a budget, but still want to enjoy tasty French food in a cozy and welcoming place can go for a restaurant called Chez Marie Louise where a full lunch menu is almost a bargain at 16 euros. Dinner might be slightly more expensive, but in any case this place is a must for anyone who likes eating in a small bistro with a warm, simple, and modern feel. Just think of tasting cod with aioli or boudin noir.

Where can you drink out in Paris? Although there are many tiny bars and pubs where you can enjoy a drink anytime, here are a couple of suggestions for people who prefer something more special.

Les Etages seems rather modest, but it serves quality drinks and the mood is romantic and very pleasant. It's located in Marais and it draws people from many parts of Paris through its warm vibe and reddish lights. Several floors where you can drink comfortably in an armchair and talk intimately with your partner. This place is perfect for couples who want to enjoy both silence and soft music in the background. Cocktails are impressive and they cost 10-11 euros.

Wine lovers can go for a more fancy place called La compagne des vins surnaturelles. As the name tells you, here you can drink high quality wine of many types and brands ... and maybe enter a surreal(ist) state of mind. Will you create some work of art a la Dali or Paul Eluard? Probably not, but you'll surely have a spectacular time in one of the most interesting places to drink out in when you visit Paris. What's totally charming about this place is the diversity of products you can find here. If you are filthy rich, you can pay even 70-80 euros for a glass of wine or thousands of euros for a whole bottle. No, this is no joke. However, this place also provides you with the opportunity to savor good French wine for 6-10 euros per glass or 20-30 per bottle. There are many types of clients who gather in this place, as you can picture. Apart from impressive drinks, this place also lures you with something to eat next to your glass of wine e.g. truffles, fine French cheese, burrata etc.

# 7. Culture and Entertainment

How can you talk about Paris without bringing up Louvre as a symbol of French culture and a priority for any tourist? Although it might be a bit difficult to "compress" such a large museum in a short visit, you might regret leaving it out or only admiring its architecture from the outside. Not that it isn't fabulous!

## Louvre

Louvre is one of the largest and most important museums in the world that includes about 35.000 pieces of art from all historical eras. It is located in the Louvre Palace which dates back to the 12the century, although its purposes were different. To top all the spectacular marvels of this museum (which is quite large and fascinating), the entry is not excessively pricey. You can visit it for 12 euros and, if you have kids who are under 17 years old, they get to join you for free. You probably already know that the Da Vinci's "Monalisa", Delacroix "Liberty Guiding the People", and Venus of Milo can be admired here. Other pieces of art created by major world artists such as Vermeer, Rembrandt, Botticelli, Ingres etc. are proudly displayed for everyone to see in this museum. If you are a passionate art lover, you'll find the Louvre heaven on earth. If you are an amateur, you will at least enjoy the chance to visit one of the top museums in the world where you can find art of many different art movements and historical times. It will be a great chance to get acquainted to some of the most valuable art objects on earth. One of the most captivating parts of the Louvre Museum is the Egyptians, an area dedicated to this antique culture that is by far the largest in the world outside Egypt. Here you can see the great statue of Ramses II, among other things.

## Musée d'Orsay

If the Louvre is "la crème de la crème" when it comes to Paris high culture, the Orsay Museum is rather "pour les connoisseurs". This museum dates back to the 19th century and it is a homage to the style of "la belle époque". It was actually a railway station (albeit an impressive one) and in the 80s it was turned into the building and cultural institution it is now. Apart from the myriad of works of art, this place displays wonderful light effects: a huge hall lets in natural light which, combined with the deliberate influence of artificial light, creates a mesmerizing picture and a unique atmosphere. This museum has a particular profile, as its collection focuses on the artistic trend known by the name of Impressionism and the related movement called Post-impressionism. If you are an art lover, you will feel extremely proud and lucky to have the opportunity to see here works by Monet, Van Gogh, Degas, Renoir etc. The top floor exhibits major pieces by renowned French impressionists, while the middle level centers on the subsequent period and artists e.g. Van Gogh, Seurat, and Gauguin. This museum can be visited at the end of a "classic" touristic day in which you've become familiar with more "universal" attractions that match everyone's interest and taste. It will prove to be an extraordinary bonus for art addicts and connoisseurs.

## Centre Georges Pompidou

This museum is a coronation of modern and postmodern art. It will strike you right from the start through its strange architecture that challenges you to understand the aesthetic particularities and goals of such a building. However the effect was definitely calculated by Renzo Piano and Richard Rogers, the architects who designed this museum in the 70s. Some people might find the architecture bizarre and even repelling; others may consider it a great work of postmodernity and tech-dominated times. Either way it's surely worth visiting this place, because it's more than a mere museum. Here you can find a library, bookshops, a cinema archive, a performance hall, a music gallery, a children's gallery etc. Only on one floor can you find the actual museum that makes this center a symbol, namely the National Museum of Modern Art. As an art addict, you'll be able to see works that belong to Dada, cubism, surrealism and others. Pieces by Picasso, Warhol, and Kandinsky and the workshop of the famous sculptor Constantin Brancusi are landmarks of this amazing museum.

## Théâtre de Champs-Elysées

People who have more free time to do various things in Paris or simply want to enjoy seeing a performance in one of the city's landmark cultural centers can choose the Champs-Elysées Theatre. This theatre is not extremely old, as it dates from the beginning of the 20th century. Its style is an attractive art deco. This building draws numerous culture lovers who belong to the city's highest class. As a tourist or a local, one has the pleasure to attend an opera show, a ballet performance, or a symphonic concert played by major philharmonic orchestras in the world.

## Palais de Tokyo

This place is the meeting space of people who are not great admirers of classic art, so to speak. This cultural center is however quite important. It usually attracts younger crowds, but also people who simply have a passion for modern and contemporary art. Here you can see many different exhibitions and attend a series of other events (which are often open till night time). Apart from art objects, one can also stop to eat something quirky in the artsy Tokyo Eat that is located in this center. The Tokyo Palace doesn't have a permanent collection, but always displays temporary events and exhibitions that are of high contemporary interest.

## Gaîeté Lirique

Another interesting cultural center you can find in Paris, this place is rather new, but very diverse and inviting. It includes a concert hall and a gallery area. This center specializes in mixed media and digital art forms. It thus attracts people from many different fields and professions who share an interest in modern culture that some people may even consider on the border between art and more pragmatic or technical things. One can even find an interactive room for video games here! This center is highly versatile and multifunctional. Depending on the time of your visit, you may find here fashion-related shows, multimedia performances, or architecture/design events. Either way this modern center is worth checking out.

## Disneyland

For people who are not high culture addicts or who simply want to enjoy something "lighter" and more amusing in the French capital, the world famous Disneyland can please even the most critical and pretentious of tourists. Is the largest theme park in the world for kids only? Not by a long shot. It's superb for adults and parents with children equally. Or at least that's what everybody says for good reason. This resort is located about 30 kilometers away from Paris and it includes hotel rooms, a shopping complex, many dining and entertainment possibilities, a golf course, and other recreational and entertainment features. As such this place is designed to satisfy many people's taste! It was open in 1992 and it prides on a large number of visitors every year.

# 8. Special Events in Paris

Probably the most famous event you can attend in the French capital is Fête de la Musique. It takes place in June and it usually involves hundreds or thousands of people who don't want only to listen to good music, but also to forget about their problems and worries and have fun like there's no tomorrow. The longest night of the year is thus celebrated with extreme euphoria. The great advantage is that you can enjoy modern music of all types for which you don't have to pay lots of cash. Bands play in pubs or on street corners. Larger open-air concerts are also a must, if you can afford enough time for this event during your stay in Paris.

A more fancy and amusing event is Paris Cocktail Week which takes place in January. This is quite a good way of keeping warm, isn't it? For a price that ranges from 8 to 12 euros, you will be able to drink many cocktail types in participating pubs and restaurants. Moreover, you'll be able to learn how to prepare cocktails yourself and how to match a cocktail with the right food. For people who enjoy drinking out and having fun in town this event is an interesting opportunity.

The Paris Carnival takes place each year in February. Reserve a few hours for wild-looking costumes, worldwide music, a parade that crosses the city singing, and a lot of enthusiasm if you visit Paris in this period. This festival may not be as famous as the ones in Brazil or Venice, but it can show you a side of Paris that you didn't know too much of.

Bastille Day is the French national celebration on the 14th of July. Lots of fireworks at the Eiffel Tower and in other strategic parts of the city, street parades, airplane shows, and many parties throughout the city are reason enough for you to visit Paris on this day.

The Long Night of Museums is nice to catch when you are a high culture lover and you need more time for seeing everything you'd like to. On the 16th of May you have the chance of visiting over 60 of the city's museums. In case you wonder if you'll have enough money for such a thing, remember that on this night everything is free. It's really worth travelling to Paris in May, isn't it? You can surely save money and see even more hidden treasures that are not always well-known to classic tourists.

Chandeleur is a more peculiar event that everyone loves. It's unique because it is dedicated to one thing only and it involved complete immersion in its delights. So what is this about? On the 2nd of February you can enjoy Crêpes Day. Doesn't that sound irresistible? On that day many restaurants and other smaller places lure people with their best offers on the menu. Various new types of crêpes were created and eaten on this day, as cuisine masters tried to bring something more original and impressive. While you can eat this typically French food on pretty much every corner of Paris streets, this day will surely make your visit more savory, spectacular and memorable.

# 9. Conclusion

This guide provided you with the necessary information and recommendations to turn your stay in Paris into a fruitful and memorable trip. As a tourist guide meant to show you what you should include in 3 days, this book aimed at combining entertainment value and cultural treasures, which is prone to satisfying many people who visit one of the world's most impressive capitals. Of course, you are also free to move the "scales" in favor of what you love most, but the premise of this short guide is that most people do want to explore both high culture and modern social delights or even more mundane attractions.

By following the suggestions in this guide, you will have a synthetic perspective on Paris that will also enable you to inform other people about what is worth seeing in this city in order to get a feel of French style, history, art, cuisine, yearly events etc. ... all at once! After you visit Paris and make use of the advice provided in this book, you will certainly be able to understand what is unique about this city and why Margaret Anderson's words are so spot-on:

"Paris is the city in which one loves to live. Sometimes I think this is because it is the only city in the world where you can step out of a railway station—the Gare D'Orsay—and see, simultaneously, the chief enchantments: the Seine with its bridges and bookstalls, the Louvre, Notre Dame, the Tuileries Gardens, the Place de la Concorde, the beginning of the Champs Elysees—nearly everything except the Luxembourg Gardens and the Palais Royal. But what other city offers as much as you leave a train?"

Printed in Great Britain
by Amazon